The Black Man's Burden

The Horrors of Southern Lynchings

By: Irenas J. Palmer

Published and Revised by: Michael L. Goines Sr.

Irenas Johnson Palmer: was born on February 20, 1842 in Hinsdale, New York. In 1863, at the age of 21 he went to Boston, Mass. to join the Fifth Regiment Massachusetts Colored Volunteer Cavalry .On December 26, 1863 he was commissioned First Sergeant.

The Fifth Regiment was involved in numerous Civil War battles at Fort Monroe, Appomattox, and Petersburg. In 1864 they were assigned to Point Lookout in Maryland where they guarded Confederate Prisoners. In 1865 they were sent to Texas because there was anticipation of trouble with Mexico.

After the Civil War in November 1865 Mr. Palmer returned to Western New York where he took up his trade as an Architect and Builder. Mr. Palmer was active in the AME Church, and the Grand Army of the Republic (GAR). He was also one of the many unknown civil rights pioneers who spoke out against injustice and the despicable criminal acts of lynching that were imposed upon countless African Americans during his lifetime. This shadow of shame inspired him to write this book in Feb. 1902.

Irenas Johnson Palmer died on June 17, 1919. He was buried at the Mount View Cemetery in Olean, NY.

We, the descendants of I.J. Palmer are honored to re-introduce, The Black Man's Burden. This book provides an insightful look into the darker side of America's history.

Michael L. Goines Sr.

PREFACE
I.J. Palmer: February 20, 1902

Fifty years ago it was not an uncommon occurrence to see in the newspapers in certain sections of our country, the picture of a colored man with a stick across his shoulder to which a bundle was attached. Below the picture would be an advertisement offering a reward for the capture and return of a runaway slave. Nor was it an uncommon occurrence to see in the papers a few days later, the account of where a fugitive slave had been overtaken, but who, having retreated into the bogs and mire of a swamp beyond the reach of the pursuing blood hounds, and refusing to surrender and return to his pursuers, had been shot dead in his tracks. Even in these latitudes the affair would create but a temporary sensation, which would disappear in a few days.

There were then men who denounced these outages and who appeal to the law-making powers for relief, but no relief was afforded. The people of this country stood before the world, darkened by the shadows of injustice and crime that pictured them as a cruel and half-civilized race.

But down in the hearts of the American people there were justice and mercy. There were the underlying principles of humanity which needed but the awakening touch, to arise with irresistible force and right the wrongs of centuries.

It is said that history repeats itself. Today we read the accounts of where colored men are shot, hanged or burned to death, and tomorrow it is forgotten. These outrages have been denounced, and the law-making powers have been appealed to for relief, but no relief has been afforded. We stand before the world as a heartless people, who permit the perpetration of cruel and fiendish crimes against man. The charge is true. But down in the souls of the people today are the principles of justice, humanity and civilization, that will someday be awakened to action and these wrongs will be righted. To this end the following pages are submitted.

The Black Man's Burden:

Kippling's celebrated poem, which appeared in the magazines some time ago, entitled "The White Man's Burden," has suggested "The Black Man's Burden" as the title of my discourse on this occasion.

Kippling says in his verse that the white nations of the world are engaged in the thankless and fruitless task of forcing civilization upon the savages. My remarks are not designed, however, as a criticism of Kippling's production. My mission is to call attention to that gory trail of lynch law that hangs out in hideous belts across every Southern State of the American republic; and which from its ulcerous and un-cleansed source, is slowly eating its way into other parts of our country; and to do the little I can towards awakening in the hearts and minds of the American people a sense of the towering injustice they are permitting; and to present the appeal of ten million colored American citizens for relief from the scourge of lawlessness, savagery and fiendishness that distresses them, which has never before been equaled in a civilized country since Nero lighted his gardens with human torches and fed Christians to lions in the arenas of Rome.

First let us see what the colored man has done that entitles him to your consideration.

One, who selects the colored man as the subject of his discourse, necessarily enters upon a broad field, and upon one whose boundaries are not well established, and whose monuments and terminals are dimmed or obscured by the corrosions of time and neglect.

The colored man, however, has been much discussed in this country. His cause has been the theme that has attracted the attention of our thinking men from the earliest inception of this government. No greater questions were encountered by the framers of our national constitution than those affecting the colored man, and none were more thoroughly debated or required greater diplomacy to present in an acceptable shape.

There were twenty-four sections in our constitution when it was adopted. Three of these sections relate to the President of the United States - his powers, privileges and duties, and three of them relate to the colored man. Fifteen sections have been added to our constitution. One of these relates to the President and three of them relate to the colored man.

During the first century of the existence of the United States government, the history of the colored man was the greater part of the political history of the country. He was the prolific source from which questions arose that often decided the fate of national and international affairs; that elected men to office or consigned them to political sepulchers; that raised men from obscurity to lofty official pinnacles, while it barred the paths along which Clay, Calhoun and Webster sought to reach the highest office within the gift of the American people. The extent to which the colored man has influenced the affairs of this country is enormous – much greater than you would imagine unless you took pains to look the matter up.

The colored man was the cause of the Missouri compromise, the Mexican war, the fugitive slave law, the Dred Scott decision, the Kansas and Nebraska struggles, and many other measures that violently agitated this country, and attracted marked attention throughout the civilized world. Laws passed by Congress affecting the colored man have been openly and defiantly nullified by the acts of State Legislatures. In proof of this statement I will present the following:

The State of South Carolina withdrew from the Union as far as she had the power, on December 20, 1860. In her ordinance of secession she set forth as the principal reason for that action the following complaint: "An increasing hostility on the part of the Free States to the institution of slavery has led to a disregard of their obligations and the laws of the general government have ceased to effect the objects of the constitution. The States of Maine, New Hampshire, Vermont, Massachusetts, Connecticut, Rhode Island, New York, Pennsylvania, Ohio, Indiana, Iowa, Wisconsin, and Michigan have enacted laws which either nullify the acts of Congress or render useless any attempt to execute them. In many of these States the fugitive is discharged from the labor claimed, and in none of them has the State government complied with the constitutional stipulations concerning fugitive slaves."

There was a good deal of truth in the complaint of South Carolina. At that time, in many of the States named, you could get a larger appropriation for the "underground railroad" than you could to enforce the provisions of the fugitive slave law. The Underground Railroad is a name that was then given to the system that facilitated the escape of men from slavery.

The colored man was the recipient of a good deal of attention in these times, but this is not all. Three of the most important amendments to the national constitution have been made in the Negro's interest. The proclamation of emancipation – properly and justly termed the peer of the Declaration of Independence – struck the fetters from four million colored bondmen; while one of the most gigantic wars of history, which drenched our land in blood and tears for four years, enforced the decree that the blighting curse of African slavery should no longer be sheltered by the American flag. The colored man is a very important factor in the affairs of our country today, as I shall show, I trust, before I get through.

From the foregoing it would seem that information relating to the career and attitude of colored men during important periods of American history would be in abundance and easy to reach. But such is not the case.

The opportunities for colored men to distinguish themselves have always been limited by reasons of caste prejudice. And while in face of all obstacles, especially in times of war, they have performed deeds that have won for them the admiration of their countrymen-deeds that have refused to be buried or to disown their authors - yet they have many times deserved credit which they have not justly received. Their commendable deeds have not generally been conspicuously marked or correctly credited by the historian or biographer, and especially is this true in the periods previous to the war of the Rebellion.

W.H. Day, in his time a strong friend of the colored man, said, way back in 1852, "Of the sufferings and services of the colored soldiers during the war of the Revolution, no attempt has, to our knowledge, been made to preserve a record. Their history is not written. It lies on the soil watered in their blood, or rests with their bones in the charnel house."

Joseph T. Wilson, the gifted author of the war record entitled "The Black Phalanx," says in his opening chapters:

"The history of the patriotic colored Americans who swelled the ranks of the colonial and continental armies has never been written; nor was any attempt made by the historians of that day to record the deeds of the colored men who dared to face death for the independence of the American colonies."

Mr. Wilson encountered many difficulties in his efforts to trace the career of the colored men through our country's wars. His search extended over a vast field and required the diligent labor of years. Not in the archives of the government did he find all that he required. Not in the histories of States, the records of battles,the correspondence of generals, or the writings and speeches of statesmen. But from all of these and from many other isolated and disconnected sources did he gather the material for the book entitled "The Black Phalanx," to which, perhaps, more than to any other single publication, we are indebted for a connected account of the deeds of colored men throughout our country's wars.

But despite the apathy, indifference or studied neglect of the Antebellum historians, there are marked deeds of loyalty, courage and intelligence, performed by colored men, that stand out prominently through the records of events, like beacon lights on a dreary coast. Deeds, as I have said, that have refused to be buried or to disown their authors - deeds that show that the colored man is ever on the side of his country, and that he freely assumes his share of the burdens essential to our country's greatness and our country's perpetuity.

In the remarks which I shall offer on this occasion I make no attempt to present anything new. I have drawn upon the labors of others for the facts which support my discourse. I shall be contented if I succeed in so presenting these facts as to furnish additional testimony that the colored man has won all the rights he enjoys, has compelled all the recognition he receives, and that he is entitled to the rights, privileges and protection which his labor has helped to secure.

The first of these facts with which we shall deal may fairly be termed the beginning of the struggle for American independence.

On the fifth of March 1770, more than one hundred and thirty years ago, and six years before the Declaration of Independence, a company of British soldiers, under the command of a Capt. Preston, were parading the streets of Boston, Mass. These troops were a part of the forces sent here by Great Britain to enforce upon the American colonies the odious and oppressive acts of the British parliament.

The presence of these troops was strongly resented by the people of this country, and every peaceful method was being employed to get rid of them.

Petitions, protests, and remonstrance had been tried and had failed. Arguments and threats were of no avail. The supplications for the redress of grievances which had been poured in upon the British throne had been answered by the relentless hand of force seeking to stamp out the spirit of human liberty which was born to this country on the free sun rays of heaven.

Though the colonies were yet under the parent rule, the camp–fires of freedom were brightly burning. The spirit of liberty was surging in every patriot's breast and the Declaration of Independence was rapidly materializing. There was a grave crisis upon the country. A resort to arms to throw off the oppressive yoke of the mother country was all that there was left, and the sturdy old patriots of that period were rapidly reaching that conclusion.

The situation was intense. It needed but a spark to fire the train. Who should apply it? Captain Preston defiantly maneuvered his troops upon the streets of Boston. Who should press the button that should start in motion determined resistance to these armed intruders?

No blood had been shed in defense of American liberties up to this time. War had reared his grim-visaged head, but his gory trail had not then started across our land. Which side should begin? Who on our side should strike the first blow?

The man for the hour was there and he struck the blow that thundered around the world – that was heard in every capital - and that is still reverberating down the centuries.

The man who struck that blow was Crispus Attucks, a Negro slave.

In that supreme moment, when patriotic indignation had thoroughly stirred the populace, Crispus Attucks, imbued with the spirit of the hour, and towering above his fellow-men in his grasp of the most effective methods, cut the Gordian knot of the dilemma, and led a host of the freedom-loving citizens of Boston upon the red-coated soldiery commanded by Captain Preston, and precipitated the conflict in which the first blood for American independence was shed, and the first sacrifices were laid upon the altars of our country's liberties.

The die was cast. The Boston harbor tea party, Lexington, Bunker Hill, the Declaration of Independence, each great and significant in itself, were logical results of a heaven-born purpose, of which the conflict on the fifth of March, 1770, was the prelude.

Crispus Attucks fell, and with him the white comrades, Gray, Cadwell, Carr and Maverick. As these heroes lay there bathed in their life's blood, the recording angel noted the birth of a new empire and the dawn of an era of progress, liberty and civilization, then unknown to the annals of history and unrevealed to the dreams of man.

The conflict was to come anyway. The spirit of liberty had become too thoroughly entrenched in the breasts of the patriotic colonists to be stamped out by the measures which Great Britain was relentlessly pursuing; but years might have elapsed before the initial stroke which electrified the country, which rekindled the fires of liberty that were slumbering and added fuel to those that were burning, would have been delivered by another hand and in another way, and our independence might have been deferred for a decade or a generation.

It required a daring and patriotic spirit to prompt the initial stroke. Perhaps it was fitting that he, who had been enslaved by his countrymen, should be the first to strike for the liberty of all.

For years afterwards the anniversary of this event was publicly commemorated by orations and other exercises. It was, in fact, treated as our national birthday till our independence was secured, when the fourth of July was substituted for the fifth of March, as a more proper day for general celebration.

A writer of the times says, concerning the conflict on the fifth of March:

"Thus the first blood for liberty which was shed in the colonies was that of a colored man, and it places him on our country's side at the very beginning of the struggle. Soon in every town and village meetings were held in which the colonists were urged to resist the oppressive and aggressive measures which the British parliament had passed, and for the enforcement of which British soldiers had drawn on the streets the patriotic blood of Boston citizens."

The feeling engendered is well shown by a speech delivered by John Hancock, of colonial fame. It was he who was first to sign the Declaration of Independence. He wrote his name beneath that document in letters two inches long, that the British and the Tories might be able to easily spell it and would have no doubts about its being there.

The speech was delivered on the spot where Attucks fell. It was on the fourth anniversary of that event. Among other things the fiery and soaring Hancock said:

"Tell me, ye bloody butchers, ye villains high and low, you wretches who contrived as well as you who executed the inhuman deed. Do you not feel the goads and stings of conscious guilt pierce through your savage bosoms? Though some of you may think yourselves exalted to a height that bids defiance to human justice, and others shroud yourselves beneath the mask of hypocrisy and build your hopes of safety on the low arts of cunning, chicanery and falsehood, yet do you not sometimes feel the gnawings of that worm that never dies? Do not the injured shades of Attucks, Gray, Cadwell, Carr and Marverick attend you in your solitary walks, arrest you in you debauches and fill even your dreams with terror?"

Daniel Webster, in his Bunker Hill oration, referring to the massacre on the fifth of March, said:

"The thirst for freedom was universal among the people of New England. With them liberty was not circumscribed by condition. And now, since the slave Attucks had struck the first blow for America's independence, thereby electrifying the colonies and putting quite a different phase upon their grievances, the people were called to witness a real slave struggling with the oppressors for his freedom. It touched the people of the colonies as they had never been touched before, and they arrayed themselves for true freedom."

John Adams, Historian Bancroft, Dr. Joseph Warren, and other prominent men, have written or spoken of the deed performed by Attucks, but we need not quote them.

The orators and writers of that time turned their eloquence upon this deed of blood and used it as a powerful and successful argument to justify and bring about the Declaration of Independence.

There were other colored heroes than Attucks who helped to achieve American independence.

A few remarks concerning the valor and intelligence of Peter Salem, another Negro slave, who was the acknowledged hero of Bunker Hill, will be presented.

The battle of Bunker Hill was clearly an American victory, though our forces were driven from the field.

The British outnumbered us three to one, and besides they had the assistance of several warships and a battery of heavy field artillery whose guns commanded the American position.

The British loss in this engagement nearly equaled the whole number of those who fought against them. The fact was there clearly demonstrated that the undisciplined Yankee was a full match for the well-drilled and well-equipped Red Coat.

The British assaulted the American position three times. They were driven back twice with great loss. Their success on the third assault was due to the fact that the continental troops had run out of ammunition. The history of the affair says:

"When the British solders came up for the third time, the American troops had been reduced to four rounds of ammunition apiece. This they reserved until the enemy were within a few rods, when it was used with great effect. The contest now, however, was too unequal to last long. The enemy soon gained the parapets.

A column led by Major Pitcairn was the first to break through. This impetuous officer, shouting that the day was won, rapidly began to move his followers into such positions as would cut off the retreat of the Americans. There was necessarily disorder and confusion, but the victorious Britons, pouring over the breastworks of the outnumbered and ammunition less Yankees, were led by trained officers who knew how to make victory complete. Major Pitcairn was cool, and he was rapidly taking advantage of the situation, when he was struck down. The hand that struck him down was that of Peter Salem, a Negro slave. The loss of Pitcairn confused the enemy and created the delay that enabled our forces to escape from the field."

Peter Salem's timely act had much to do with averting the disaster that threatened our forces at Bunker Hill.

It is not my design to dwell upon the deeds of daring and valor performed by colored soldiers during the struggle for this country's liberty. There were many of them-enough to fill volumes with their accounts. I have presented the above well authenticated instances to show where colored men stood at the very beginning of the contest for American freedom. Crispus Attucks, Peter Salem, Ebenezer Hill, Samuel Slater, Daniel Warner, John Fruman, are the names of a few of the many colored soldiers, who in the face of prejudice and other obstacles, and without the incentive of promotion or other reward, earned marked distinction for deeds of gallantry and valor in the wars that gave us the American Republic.

Colored soldiers under Gates, under Lafayette, under Washington, and other leaders in the revolution; colored soldiers at Bennington, Saratoga, Valley Forge and York Town; colored soldiers in the army and navy, contributed their full share of the courage and the sufferings that were necessary to win in the struggle that was started on the streets of Boston on the memorable fifth of March, 1770.

The dusky arms that struck so valiantly for the Union cause deserved better treatment than they received at the hands of the dominant classes when our independence was secured. The constitution, which was adopted by this country, had no reward for the black man. It secured no rights of citizenship to the colored soldier who fought or to the descendants of him who died upon the battle fields of the revolution. But the constitution said that the African slave trade should be protected by law for a third of a century after the Declaration of Independence. It said that the poor colored man, guilty of no offense whatever, should be a hunted outlaw and legitimate prey for the blood-hound and the rifle of his pursuer, and that the whole country must organize to hunt him down. It said that the black man had no rights which a white man is bound to respect, except the right to be counted at the ballot box, while somebody else cast the ballot. Such is the organic law with which the white man burdened this country at its start, and under which it grew during the first eighty years of its existence. Such is the gratitude manifested towards a weak and scanty people for their courage and suffering during eighty years of sanguinary struggle, to establish the principle, that all men are created equal with the inalienable rights of life, liberty and the pursuit of happiness.

Is it any wonder that a day of reckoning came? Is it any wonder that a million graves and billions of dollars was the price demanded for this terrible blunder? But retribution was sure then and it is now. The injustices and outrages that go unpunished today will yield their legitimate fruit, and somewhere along the line the account must be settled.

Colored men took a hand in the war of 1812. One of the events that brought on that war was the forcible taking of some colored men from an American vessel by a British cruiser, and impressing them into the British service.

Great Britain claimed the right to search American vessels for alleged British deserters. The young republic would rather fight than suffer such indignities. Great Britain disregarded our ultimatum and the second war followed.

But colored men were not received into the Union armies at the beginning of the struggle. I can safely say that on the other side of the battle of Appomattox this country has never squarely received the services of colored soldiers till driven to it by absolute necessity.

When the war of 1812 began this was a white man's government and that was a white man's war. It was not long, however, before the government began to modify that attitude. When the commonwealth of Maine had been wrested from our control; when the national capital had been burned; when our forces were threatened with annihilation, a change came over the spirit of their dreams.

The country called on the colored man for help. The State of New York and other states authorized the arming of Negro troops and General Jackson made a strong appeal to the colored men of Louisiana to arise and to assist him to repel the invasion of Packenham and his army of

Wellington's trained veterans. And from every side the colored man responded with patriotic alacrity.

Colored soldiers constituted more than one-eighth of the forces that enabled General Jackson to win the decisive battle of New Orleans, the last struggle of the white man's government in the white man's war of 1812.

How well the colored soldier deported himself in that conflict is shown by General Jackson's proclamation of thanks.

This proclamation can be found in the national library, Niles Register, Volume II. I quote from it as follows:

"Proclamation. To the men of color; Soldiers, from the shores on Mobile: I collected you to arms. I invited you to share in the perils and divide the glory of your white countrymen. I expected much from you for I was aware that you possessed qualities that render you formidable to an invading foe. I knew that you could endure hunger and thirst, and all of the hardships of war. I knew you loved the land of your nativity, and like ourselves had to defend all that is most dear to man. But you have surpassed my expectations. I have found in you united to these qualities that noble enthusiasm that impels to great deeds. Soldiers, the President of the United States shall be informed of your conduct on this occasion, and the voice of the representatives of American nation shall applaud your valor as your General now praises your ardor."

The above proclamation is pretty good evidence that colored men were then doing something for this country and its institutions.

Colored men fought in other battles than that of New Orleans, and very remarkably so in Commodore Perry's battles on Lake Erie. But I shall not dwell on these, and I shall pass the Mexican war without remark. I will now come down to more recent times and review some of the events that are still fresh in the memory of thousands yet living.

The year 1863, the third year of the rebellion, was ushered in amid grave misgivings. The stoutest patriot shuddered as he contemplated the probable destruction of the American Union. War had spread his blighting effects far and wide and had stationed his grim spectre at almost every fireside. The poetry of battle had vanished; its horrors and suffering were invading every household.

Reverses had fallen upon our armies; the national credit was low down in the scale of quotations; there were the croaking of copperheads and the exultations of enemies. The dismal clouds of doubt and distress hung like a funeral pall across American skies. The citizen, the soldier, the statesman, were conscious of our peril.

England, France, Europe, hovered in the distance like vultures awaiting their prey. The world stood in suspense as the cause of liberty and progress and the life of this great nation trembled in the balance.

In that hour of dark forebodings, when hope drooped from her pinnacle; when the fruitless struggle of Antietam followed by the terrible reverse at Fredericksburg, had discouraged enlistments in the Northern armies, and had made conscription unpopular to the extent of open resistance; in that dark hour the white man's cry went up, "oh Lord! Our burden is greater than we can bear." In that terrible hour the national cry went out to the colored man, "Take up the white man's burden, rescue the American flag from dishonor and destruction and preserve the integrity of the American Union." What was the answer?

The cry was heard and answered; and in twelve months two hundred thousand colored men sprang to its response, turned defeat into victory, and saved intact the flag that shelters you and him today.

It is a good deal to say - a good deal to claim for our people, that with the American eagle driven from his perch a fugitive in hiding; that with the glorious old banner being robbed of its stripes and being despoiled of its stars, the great government of the United States, on the verge of destruction, turned to its colored patriots with a prayer for help that it might not die.

But it did; and despite the wrongs and prejudices we had suffered; despite the fact that colored soldiers were at first paid much less than their white comrades and barred from all lines of promotion; despite the crowning infamy of two hundred and fifty years of slavery which was actually sustained by the Union soldiers restoring to their masters the escaped slave, the colored men responded. And in loyal throngs, from every corner of the land, faster than the government could arm and equip, they flocked to the Union standard, singing that patriotic refrain, "We are coming, Father Abraham, three hundred thousand more."

And from the red soil of Virginia; from the contested hills of Tennessee; from the victorious fields of Georgia, they sent up that determined cry that was wafted on the winds of Heaven to every corner of the globe; that echoed and re-echoed its warning notes through the halls and corridors of the Courts of St. James and the Courts of Paris; that shouted consternation to treason; sang the dirge of rebellion and sounder the death knell of African slavery; that welcomed – that world-awakening message, "We will stand by the American flag through a million of us fall in its defense.

And they stood there. In that needed-that indispensable hour the colored man came, and bared his breast to cruel war. And striking for the Union, for our country, and the flag; amid the terrible storms of fire and iron hail he sank torn and bleeding on many of our country's blood-drenched battle fields, with his eyes towards heaven and his feet to the foe.

It is a good deal to say, I repeat, that in that dark hour the of this great nation hung on the thread of the colored man's valor and the colored man's loyalty, but the cold facts are there; they have been stamped upon the historic page of our country by the indelible hand of war.

The historian shall yet write that but for courage and valor of colored men during the war of the rebellion, the Star Spangled Banner could not today float unchallenged from the Lakes to the Gulf, from the Atlantic to the Pacific; from the tropical waters of the Rio Grande to the ice-clad peaks of Alaska. Could not float from the summits of Porto Rico and usher God's free sun rays upon the eastern shores of the western world; could not from the mountain tops of the Philippines herald the dawn of day to the sleeping millions of the Orient; could not set in the skies of the globe that never-ending, never-fading and ever-visible rainbow, composed of thirteen bands and forty-five stars, carrying courage to the weak; carrying civilization into darkness, and shedding gold and silver tints upon the dismal clouds that overhang the oppressed.

From 1776 to the battle of Appomattox the government of the United States was an experiment. On the ninth of April, 1865, the American Republic graduated. She placed her name in the roll book of nations; cast her banner upon the tidal wave of progress, and firmly put her shoulder to the burdens of civilization. Call it the white man's burden if you will, but Appomattox was not wholly a white man's triumph.

When the experiment of colored troops had been tried and had proven successful; when confidence in the eventual success of the Union forces had regained its hold in the minds of the people; when the victorious shouts of our advancing armies had restored hope to loyal hearts, President Lincoln, looking over the results of an experiment which he had entered upon with doubts and reluctance, spoke as follows to Judge Mills of Wisconsin, a pro-slavery advocate, who had come to remonstrate against the employment of colored troops. Mr. Lincoln said:

"The slightest knowledge of figures will prove to anyone that the rebel armies cannot be destroyed by democratic strategy. It would sacrifice all of the white men of the North to do it. There are now in the service of the United States near two hundred thousand colored men - the most of them under arms defending and acquiring Union territory. The democratic strategy demands that these forces be disbanded, and that the masters be conciliated by returning those that were slaves to bondage. The black men who now assist Union prisoners to escape are to be converted into our enemies in the vain hope of gaining the good will of their masters. We shall have to fight two nations instead of one. You cannot conciliate the South if you guarantee them ultimate success, and the experience of the present struggle proves that their success is inevitable if you force millions of colored men on to their side of the fight. Will you give our enemies such advantages as insures success, and then depend on coaxing and flattery and concessions to get them back into the Union? If we abandon all the posts now garrisoned by colored troops, and take two hundred thousand men from our side and put them into the battlefield or cornfield against us, we would be compelled to abandon the war in three months."

No stronger testimony is needed to conclusively prove how indispensable the colored soldier was to the preservation of the Union. There is no better authority than that of President Lincoln. But I will give more of that interview. Mr. Lincoln continued:

"We have to hold territory in sickly and inclement places. Where are the democrats to do it? It was a free fight and the field was open to the war democrats to put down this rebellion by fighting against both master and slave long before the present policy was inaugurated. There have been men base enough to ask me to return to slavery the black warriors of Olustee and Port Hudson, and thus win the respect of the masters they fought. Should I do so I should deserve to be dammed in time and eternity. Come what will, I will keep my faith with friend and foe. My enemies pretend that I am now carrying on this war for the purpose of abolition. So long as I am President it shall be carried on for the sole purpose of restoring the Union. But no human power can subdue the rebellion without the use of the present policy."

There is the testimony of the foremost man on the globe at that time. There are thousands that know that it is the exact truth.

The fact is not disputed that the tide of war in the most critical period of the rebellion was turned in favor of the Union cause by the solid, loyal front of American colored men.

By their voice all over the land; by their votes where they could vote; on the Union fortifications; on the plantation giving aid to escaping Union prisoners or furnishing information to Union generals; or in the field firmly facing the terrors of war, they were ever found on the right side, on the side of our country and the flag, and they were there when a supreme crisis demanded their help.

I shall make no attempt to recite the deeds of heroism performed by colored soldiers during the war of the rebellion. Olustee, Port Hudson, Wilderness, Petersburg, and many other historic battles, are still fresh in the memory of thousands yet living. No braver men ever laid down their lives in their country's defense than were numbered among the colored slain on those hotly contested fields.

We do not claim that the colored soldier did all of the fighting, or most of the fighting, or the best of the fighting. But we do claim, and we have shown beyond successful contradiction, that the colored soldier was a necessary auxiliary to the Union forces, and that he freely threw his weight into the balance, when his weight was a necessity to insure the success of the Union cause.

There were white men and colored men who were at that time bearing the burden in Kippling's picture; but there were only white men fighting against them.

Now there are other contests than those of war. We come up against grave emergencies in which courage and intelligence are needed on other lines than those of physical force. Governments are often menaced by other enemies than those of armed foes within or without.

The problem of successful government requires the highest order of intelligence for its solution. Especially is this true of republics where the rulers come fresh from the people every few years, and the policies of the government are affirmed or condemned by the voice of the masses quite as often.

In this country we frequently see remarkable and quite contradictory changes of policy, directed by the people, in comparatively short periods of time. By way of illustration, I present the following:

In 1890 this country was in favor of a protective tariff. It was also in favor of purchasing seven tons of silver every day in the year to be coined into money. In 1892, by unmistakable majorities, we voted for free trade. In 1893 we condemned and repealed the silver policy of three years before. In 1894, by phenomenal majorities, we condemned the free trade policy which had just seen the light. In 1896 we restored the protective tariff. And so on and so on.

In 1896 we were confronted with another question, freighted with an importance which will be thoroughly comprehended only in the years to come. The grave question was presented, should this country keep on the high and progressive plain, with reference to sound money, which has become one of its time-honored traditions; or should we start on the retrograde path and lower our standard to the level of Mexico, China and Tripoli - a level which even the civilization of Peru and Japan are climbing above.

The question was decided, and the victory that was achieved was second only to York Town in the revolution and Appomattox in the rebellion. How did the colored man deport himself in this conflict?

The great presidential election of 1896 was decided by the colored voters of this country. A pretty big statement, but I will show you that it is true.

The case is well outlined by an article which appeared in the Washington Post a few weeks after the election of 1896. The post said:

"At every stage of his personal fight, Mr. McKinley has been indebted to the Negro. It was the Negro contingent at St. Louis that made his nomination certain. It was the colored delegates' firm stand for gold that forced the sound money issue upon the convention. It was the Negro vote in many States that made Republican victory possible. We all know now that Mr. McKinley would have had next to no chance at all had not the St. Louis convention declared emphatically and unequivocally for the gold standard. It was the solid sound-money front presented by the colored delegates that compelled the adoption of the gold clause in the platform and furnished Mr. McKinley with the issue upon which he rallied to his banner the merchant, the manufacturer and the great business interests throughout the land. Mr. McKinley could not have been elected but for the course pursued by the Negroes before, during and after the assembling of the St. Louis convention."

In support of the Post's statement, I will quote a few figures of the returns of the election in 1896. My figures are from the World Almanac of 1897.

"President McKinley's majority in the electoral college of 1897 was ninety-five. The States of California, Delaware, Indiana, Maryland, Ohio, Oregon, Kentucky and West Virginia were carried for Mr. McKinley by the colored voters. A majority of the white voters in every one of these States went for Mr. Bryan, but the colored voters were numerous enough to carry them the other way. These eight States sent eighty electors to the electoral college. Seventy-eight of these electors voted for Mr. McKinley. Had only thirty-two of them voted for him he would have been defeated.

The popular and electoral vote for the presidential election of 1896 can be found on page 423, World Almanac, of 1897, and on page 376 can be found the colored male population of voting age in the several States. With this data you can easily verify the figures which I here submit.

"A change of 1400 votes in California would have given that State to Mr. Bryan. A small part of her colored voters could have caused the change. One-third of Delaware's 8,000 colored voters could easily have destroyed Mr. McKinley's plurality of 3,600 in that State. A change of 9,100 votes in Indiana would have placed that State in the Bryan column. Indiana had over 13,000 colored voters. Kentucky's 60,000 colored voters are clearly responsible for Mr. McKinley's small plurality there in 1896.

The great State of Ohio could have been carried the other way in Mr. McKinley's first election by less than 24,000 of her voters. Thirty-one thousand colored men voted in Ohio. In the same election 17,000 votes could have changed the result in Maryland, but 50,000 colored men cast their ballots there on that occasion. Ten thousand colored voters in Oregon; 2,000 plurality for sound money. West Virginia had over 10,000 colored voters. Had 6,000 of them voted for Mr. Bryan he would have carried that State in 1896.

Such is the record made by the colored men in 1896 on the great question of sound money. We submit it for criticism and history. We fully appreciate the substantial endorsement which this attitude has received at the hands of the American voter after considering this question for four years.

The instances to which I have called your attention, while perhaps among the more important, are but a few of the many where the colored man has shown his devotion to his country in its hour of trial. It is one of the characteristics of the race. Whatever may be said about their intellectual inferiority, or about the degenerating influences of two hundred and fifty years of slavery; no colored American needs to peruse, with chagrin, the record made by his people when our country's interest has been at stake, and when prompt and intelligent action has been needed in our most critical periods.

Such loyalty – such devotion cannot go unrewarded. It is not consistent with the practice and teachings of a Christian age.

As we look back across the stretch of time and draw comparisons, we shall see that the colored man is getting his reward through it be in the shape of tardy and only partial justice.

Less than one hundred years ago our laws tolerated the African slave trade. That was stopped. The fighters for the rights of man were gaining ground. The Missouri compromise of more than three-quarters of a century ago was but a partial lull in the irrepressible conflict. The fugitive slave law and the Dred Scott decision were but idle commands for the sea of events to turn back. The world was advancing along the lines of civilization; and progress and light could form no partnership with that relic of barbarism, African slavery.

The salve power correctly read the handwriting on the wall. Its logical deductions were that the infernal institution was doomed; but like all expiring monsters it struck out wildly, and in its ravings it demanded and obtained of a cringing and intimidated constituency the fugitive slave law, the Dred Scott decision, and the acts of secession.

The turning point was inevitable, and it came. The election of Abraham Lincoln, the conflict of 1860, the proclamation of emancipation, the amendments to the constitution, the acts of reconstruction, all followed in rapid succession. The frantic efforts of the slave power to perpetuate its existence had failed.

A century has made a great change in this country. In 1807 our flag sheltered the African slave trade. In 1807 the slaver, flaunting at its mast-head the Stars and Strips, rode the waters of the Potomac; and anchoring in the shadows of the national capital, discharged its cargo of manacled human beings who had been torn from their native shores by pirates bearing a legal commission from the government of the United States.

In 1805 Thomas Jefferson was inaugurated President of the United States. He took the oath of office in the National capital, but within sight of the slave pen and the auction block, and within hearing of the crack of the driver's whip, the baying of the blood hounds, the clinking of the handcuffs and the groans of the victims.

No free colored man witnessed the inaugural ceremonies on that occasion. No colored man dared to stand up and assert his manhood, and demand the rights which God had designed for him. Few were the white men who dared to plead the black man's cause under the dome of the National Capitol.

We need not go back to 1805. We need go back only half of that distance. There are men living today who have seen the slave catcher; who have sheltered the fugitive; who have been agents of the Underground Railroad. There are men yet living who have seen the poor Negro, guilty of no offense whatever, torn by the merciless jaws of the blood hound, or fall a victim to the deadly rifle of his pursuer. There are men yet living who have heard from the steps of the National Capitol, the hoarse callings of the auctioneer, as he sold human beings into slavery, mingling his tones with the speeches of congressmen who were enacting laws for the land of the free and the home of the brave. Inside of fifty years have all these things taken place. But I go back to 1805, because, when at the inauguration in that year, the Chief Justice of the United States administered the oath of office to Thomas Jefferson, the

President swore to enforce the statutes that made it lawful for piratical crafts to seize colored men on the coast of Africa and bring them to this country, consigned to cruel and life-long slavery.

The colored man did not have many rights then. No one boasted of the sacrifices he had made in their behalf. But a century has made a great change in their condition in this country.

In 1896 a citizen of the United States is elected to the office of President. In 1897 he is inaugurated. He is placed at the head of the greatest nation on earth and is inducted to the greatest office mortal can enter.

As he takes the oath of office no bondman's moan distresses the occasion; but thousands of colored American citizens witness the impressive ceremonies.

Colored citizens, colored office-holders, colored legislators, colored congressmen, assist in the proceedings, and the multitude look upon a president who was nominated by colored delegates, elected by colored voters, inaugurated by the help of colored citizens, and who swore to defend the constitution of a free people upon a Bible presented for the occasion by the colored Christians of the country.

Surely the colored man's cause is advancing. From out of the depths of a cruel and oppressive past he is slowly but surely stepping into the sunlight of God's freedom.

But even now as we review the picture – this tribute to the civilization of the Western Hemisphere – this vast improvement upon a condition that has existed – we shudder as we contemplate the lawlessness, the savagery, the fiendishness, that stalks abroad unchallenged in a vast portion of the American Republic today.

We are filled with horror as we hear the anguishing cries that come up from more than fifty thousand graves filled with the bodies of colored victims who have fallen at the hands of Southern law-breakers since the close of the war of the rebellion.

And then we are told that the great government of the United States, able and willing to stretch forth its strong arm in defense of Cuba; ready to sally forth like the Knights of old in quest of the grievances of others to redress; sending vast armies across twelve thousand miles of ocean in the interest of law, order and civilization; is powerless to stay the hand of the Southern desperado, who, with impunity, shoots, hangs or burns innocent and defenseless colored men, in the light of the noonday sun, and under the very domes of the court houses. Unable to arrest that fiendishness, never equaled in the darkest hour of the Spanish occupation of the new world, and absolutely revolting to the lowest savages of the Philippine group.

The government that promptly pays indemnity when Italians or Chinamen are murdered here, cannot even protest against the illegal and unconcealed killing of its own citizens.

And this is our government today. Fifty thousand victims of cold blooded murder and no redress. The ghastly work going steadily on, and no signs of redress. If this is our government, in Gods name let us seek to make it better. Let us take up the black man's burden. Let us send forth from the colored press the colored pulpit, the colored rostrum; yes, from the housetops and the ballot box, a continuous and vigorous torrent of protests, remonstrances and boycotts, till we arouse to action that sense of justice that ever permeates the American people; and till we start coursing through the veins of the nation the progressive currents of law, justice and civilization.

Let us seek to rescue our country from a condition found nowhere else on the globe, not in Spain, not in Turkey, not in China; not even in the savage tribes of Africa or America do people commit such revolting murder, in open day, without hindrance or without inquiry. Of all organized governments the United States is the only one where ruthless savages may mutilate, may shoot, may hang, may burn to death its citizens without fear of punishment.

The black man's burden is unceasing effort for the suppression of this monumental iniquity.

We are told that punishing the crime of murder is a State affair, and the general government has nothing to do with it. Such is not the case. There are ample powers in Congress delegated to it by the constitution, to deal with this question. Time will not permit me to more than glance at this subject.

The Fifth Amendment to the Constitution prescribes that no person shall be deprived of life without due process of law. The sole object of this clause is to protect the lives of the people.

A due process of law is, among other things, a sufficient inquiry, before or after, to clearly show the cause of every death of an inhabitant with a view of reducing these causes to a minimum.

If a man dies of a disease, a doctor's certificate presumes the inquiry has been made. If a man is killed in an accident, the coroner's inquest is generally sufficient. If a man is murdered, the coroner's inquest is the inquiry; but the due process of law demands the existence of law for the punishment of murder and a reasonable effort to enforce it.

That article of the constitution to which I have called your attention, clearly includes all of the above cases, as well as the cases where men are deprived of life by direction of the law. The difference is that the first named cases are post mortem processes, while the last named case is an ante-mortem process.

If a man, without a legal trial, be put to death by the direction of a Governor of a State in his official capacity, it is clearly a case of depriving a man of life without due process of law. We can hardly deny the right of the general government to investigate such cases and to make such laws as will tend to prevent the recurrence of such affairs.

But it is said that men are not killed that way. This is generally true. But if a man is murdered and neither the Governor nor any of his subordinates take any steps to apprehend and punish the criminal, how do we know that these officers did not aid or abet the commission of the crime, and how can we know without an investigation, and who but the general government is to investigate?

If a man is murdered, and neither the Governor, the sheriff, nor the district attorney, take any steps to catch and punish the offenders, these officers are accessory to the crime. Accessory after the fact, perhaps, and possibly only to the extent of neglecting their duty, but accessories just the same, and it is the duty of the general government to investigate and to ascertain to what extent they are accessories, and to pass the laws that will best remedy the evil.

If a man is lynched by a mob of criminals who are not all residents of the same state, it becomes an interstate affair; and it is not disputed that the general government has jurisdiction. But how are we to know when these desperadoes cross State lines on their murderous mission? Only by a national law that shall direct the government officers to investigate any case of lynching, to ascertain where the law-breakers live, for the purpose of deciding the question of jurisdiction.

When the time comes that the officers of the government shall go down and investigate these deeds of murder, and compel the members of the chivalrous mob, flushed with the glory of having just burned a poor defenseless colored man at the stake, to furnish satisfactory evidence that they are all residents of the same State, a great deal will have been done towards eradicating the blackest stain that besmears our civilization today. There is a way to reach this evil. There are ample powers in Congress to deal with this question.

The Fifth Amendment to the constitution prescribes that no person shall be deprived of life without due process of law. The same amendment also prescribes that private property shall not be taken for public use without just compensation. The same amendment prescribes that no person shall be compelled to be a witness against himself. It further prescribes that no person shall be tried for crime except upon an indictment. This same amendment also prescribes that no person shall be twice put in jeopardy of life or limb for the same offense.

Every one of the above provisions, except the first named, is duly respected, and is enforced by laws passed by Congress. What argument can be advanced that will except the first named provision from the same treatment?

Let us glance at the Post Office department and see what Congress can do under very limited instructions from the constitution.

"The Congress shall have power to establish post offices and post routes."

This is all there is in the constitution about our complex postal system. Twelve words cover the whole ground. But twelve volumes would not contain the laws that have been created and that maintain the post office department of the United States.

Congress has taken hold of this matter. It has passed the laws that make the transmission and distribution of the mails as secure and effective in Louisiana or Texas, as they are in New York or Massachusetts.

If a man obstructs the transmission of the mails in Arkansas, the government officers promptly hunt up the obstructer and punish him. If a man robs the mail in Georgia, he is arrested and sent to prison by the government. If you send obscene or profane matter through the mails, you are arrested by government officers and are tried in government courts.

And all of this power is derived from the twelve-worded article – The Congress shall have power to establish post offices and post routes.

If you send an obscene letter to your neighbor, the government officers will pounce down upon you and take you to jail; but if you go over and kill that neighbor, the general government is powerless to interfere, though no person shall be deprived of life without due process of law, is the plain command of the constitution.

The remedy for this deplorable and incongruous state of affairs lies wholly with Congress. That body has legislated for the post office and the post route; but it has signally failed to develop the germs of our organic law that are designed to protect the lives of the people.

We come to Congress with the burden of our complaint. We ask that body to pass the laws that effect the objects of the constitution. We know it will invite criticism, opposition and denunciation. We know that a wave of howls will roll across certain sections of our land. But the issue is to be met - the battle is to be fought – and justice and mercy are opposed to delay.

And when Richard Roe, who represents a law-abiding constituency, gets up in his place in Congress and introduces such a measure; and when he points out that it is designed to stay the red hand of assassination; to stop the frightful slaughter of colored people, already exceeding fifty thousand victims; to arrest the revolting practice of burning human beings at the stake, making the occasion a holiday, with excursions on the railroads; I want to hear the member who sets up the howl that the general government is invading the sacred prerogatives of the great State of Texas.

When Richard Row further points out that armed packs of cowards, numbering from fifty to five hundred; not one of whom would dare to meet a colored man in equal combat, assemble in the stealth of night, and sneak down upon an unarmed and solitary colored family; and set fire to the house; and when the father, aroused from his midnight slumber by the hissing tongues of flame, the crackling of burning walls, the screeches of wife and children, catches his dear ones in his arms and rushes from the crumbling structure; he and his children go down to death beneath the deadly volley of a hundred cowardly shot guns. And while the widowed, the wounded, the bereaved wife, surrounded by a pack of howling, blaspheming brutes, kneel in the flickering lights of her destroyed home, and raises both hands aloft and prays, "Oh, pitying Father in Heaven, save my husband, save my children," the leader of that mob rushers upon that frail, defenseless, pleading form, and with an inhuman blow hurls her, stunned and bleeding to the earth, by the side of her dead husband and dying children. A half hour later she recovers. And amid the terrible solitude of her desolate surroundings, she presses the cold hand of her assassinated husband and the cold cheeks of her murdered children; and then she swoons and sinks again to the ground, reddened by the blood of all on earth that is dear to her.

This is no overdrawn picture. No pen – no tongue can fully portray these horrors. Baker, the colored man, while escaping from his burning home, at midnight, with his children in his arms, went down to death in the way I have described. His sole offense was daring to receive the commission from the President of the United States to be postmaster in a South Carolina town.

The perpetrators of this terrible deed, though known, and known to be guilty, were never punished. There was a trial, and so clearly was guilt established that not even all of that South Carolina jury could be intimidated to the extent of voting an acquittal. The jury disagreed.

It was then within the province of the general government – the prosecutor – to bring another trial; and if needed, in another section of the country. But it was not done. The one grand opportunity to place the nation's stamp of condemnation upon the horrible crimes of the lynchers was not embraced. The story of this unrebuked outrage, like thousands of others, went forth on its fiendish mission to encourage other murders; and to contribute its hellish quota to that dastardly deed which, on the 6th of September, 1901, spread a cloud of grief, misery and mourning over a nation of eighty million souls.

The anarchist and the lyncher are of the same genus. Both are foes of law and order. Both are human fiends. But they are of different species. The anarchists treat the law with contempt. He strikes at those in high places and commits his diabolical crimes with a fanatical courage that makes no attempt to escape the results.

The lyncher, in his cowardice, attacks only the weak and defenseless; and builds his hopes of escape upon concealment, perjury and intimidation, and the helpless condition of the class from which he selects his victims.

In this country it is unsafe to be black or be President. In this great country they burn colored men at the stake and one third of its Presidents are murdered by assassins. No other country on the globe can present such a showing.

There is something to be done here. We have got to put our foot down upon murder in all of its shapes. We must stamp out the anarchist and we must stamp out the lyncher. The conditions under which one can flourish will foster and develop the other.

We must have laws that will stay the hand of the treacherous anarchist who seeks the life of the head of the nation, and we must have laws that will suppress the lawless mob that applies the midnight torch to the unsuspecting residence of a colored family, and then cowardly shoots down the occupants as they rush from the blazing home.

When Richard Roe points out the horrors that his bill is designed to suppress, I want to hear the member who defends these cowardly mobs, who extols their courage and praises their chivalry; and who shrieks forth the warning notes that the centralizing tendencies of the general government are menacing the cherished State rights of South Carolina.

It is claimed, and there is still a remnant of the vanishing belief, that there is a measure of justification for many of the outrages of which colored people are the victims. I will spare your patience by dealing with this part of my subject briefly.

Before the war the colored man was all right. During the war while the white men were away in armies of Lee and Johnson, no charges were brought against the Negroes; but directly after the war the frightful slaughter of colored people began – the penalty of loyalty and liberty.

And when the world demanded an explanation, they said it was the result of race riots and Negro insurrections. But no Negro rioter was ever apprehended and only colored men were killed in the insurrections. The white men always escaped unharmed.

The race riot excuse demanded and obtained thousands of victims, but at length it wore itself out. The outrages increased however.

Negro domination was the next excuse; and for more than a decade this legend was painted upon the sanguinary banners of Southern savages with innocent blood of thousands of colored people. The world at length learned that this excuse was an imposture and it was abandoned.

Assault upon white women was next invented. Humanity abhors the assailant of womanhood, and this charge upon the Negro at once placed him beyond the pale of human sympathy.

But the charge was and is false, and the Southern chivalry know it. The southern Negro is no worse now in this respect than he was in the days of slavery and in the days of the war. He is no worse in this respect than is the northern Negro, or the northern or southern white man; but it has required a long and gory campaign of mob law and assassination, stretching across nearly two decades to convince the thinking people of the Christian world that this charge is false.

This excuse is about worn out. Today the southern murderer does not always trouble himself to offer any excuse for his crimes. He don't have to. He just kills a colored person – man, woman or child – whenever he gets ready, and that is all there is about it.

The fact is well established that there is now or has been no measure of justification for the long and ghastly career of the dirk, the halter, the stake and the shotgun, that disfigures with its hideous blotches the civilization of the Western Republic.

Yet reeking with slaughter, infamous with assassination, this ghastly parade passes steadily in review, before the eyes of the government and the nation; keeping time to the anguishing cries that come up from fifty thousand graves, whose victims have been fed to the insatiable monster of Southern lawlessness without so much as a vigorous protest from the general government, or even the promise of a vigorous protest.

This terribly diseased condition demands attention and remedy, and we come to Congress as the proper physician to prescribe for the malady.

Not every colored man is a good man. There are black men as low, as brutish, as fiendish, as it is possible for human beings to be. Black men have committed crimes for which there is no adequate physical punishment. The same is equally true of white men, and of every other race of people on the globe.

Lynch law is the poorest kind of remedy for this disease. Lynch law is a trace of barbarism, an inspiration of cowardice; and it punishes without investigation, without evidence and without guilt. Lynch law teaches and inspires savagery and disregard of law; it encourages brutality and violence, and marks the retrograde of civilization.

That terrible spectacle of chaining a human being to an iron stake, and then saturating his clothing and his person with inflammable oil, and then piling combustible materials about his feet. Then a dissolute, brazen-faced female, falsely posing as an assaulted victim, with perjury and murder in her heart; with one hand clutching the thirty pieces of blood money, with the other she applies the fatal match that envelopes a human being in the terrible agonies of smoke, fire and death. This has been done in the land of the Southern chivalry.

If the chivalry can show by the records of legal courts, that a fraction of what they charge against the colored man is true, the whole country will join them in the hue and cry against such monsters. But they will not attempt such a showing. They don't want the light of investigation turned upon their methods of iniquity. They don't want the world to know how many of their assaulted white women are willing parties to the nameless deed.

I will quote a single instance by way of illustration: "In Texarkana, Ark., Edward Coy was accused of assaulting a white woman. The press dispatches of Feb. 18, 1892, told in detail how he was tied to a tree, the flesh cut from his body by men and boys, and after oil was poured over him, the woman he had assaulted applied the match. Fifteen thousand persons saw him burn to death. On the 1st of October, 1893, the Chicago Inter – Ocean contained the following account of the horror, from the pen of Judge Albion W. Tourgee, as the result of his investigation:

1st. The woman who was paraded as the victim of violence was of bad character. Her husband was a drunkard and a gambler.

2nd. She was publicly reported and generally known to have been criminally intimate with Coy for more than a year.

3rd. She was compelled by threats, if not by violence, to make the charges against the victim.

4th. When she came to apply the match Coy asked her if she would burn him after they had been sweet-hearting so long.

5th. A large majority of the white men prominent in the affair are the reputed fathers of mulatto children.

The members of the Southern chivalry cannot prove the charges they make against colored men, they know they are false. They know that nine-tenths of the Southern lynchings are due to jealousy, race hatred, prejudice and lawlessness.

One of the glittering exponents of Southern chivalry, whose innate anarchism and seething lynching proclivities and brazen boasts of wanton murder are his sole claims to notice from the American people, has recently sent out the word that a thousand more colored people are to be lynched a thousand more human beings are to be shot, hanged or burned to death by Southern mobs, solely because the President of the United States entertained Booker T. Washington as a guest at the White House.

This work has already begun. In South Carolina the chivalry has already commenced. According to recent press dispatches, white men, blacked up and otherwise disguised as colored men, commit crimes which the lynchers speedily avenge upon the colored men whom the chivalry has marked as their victims.

The Southern lynchers stand ready to carry out this bloody decree, and a thousand more ready-made and shelf-worn cases of heinous crimes committed by colored men, are to be unpacked and distributed through the land to excuse this slaughter of a thousand people.

A thousand more mobs are to assemble with ropes and shot guns and iron stakes and chains and kerosene oil; and a thousand more victims are to be tortured to death with a fiendishness which the devil himself would denounce as atrocious.

Some may be guilty, but many will be innocent. Some will be accused; some will not even be charged with crimes. There will be no trial, no investigation, no evidence. A mob, a victim, and a savage murder in every instance. That is all.

There will come a change. When or in what way no one, now, may be able to say; but it will surely come.

The mills of God grindly slowly, but they grind exceedingly fine.

There will come a time when the laws will convict and when the laws will punish; when the laws will convict and punish all alike. When this time comes the great Negro problem is settled, and it is not settled till then.

There is no excuse for these dastardly deeds of Southern lynchers. The laws are made and executed by the white men, and let them be stringent and be promptly and vigorously enforced. We ask for no measure that will shield crime or delay the execution of justice.

There is not much danger that a colored man in the South will escape deserved punishment at the hands of judges and juries made up of a people who encourage mob violence, condone assassins and palliate the lynching of colored American citizens.

No greater questions than these demand the attention of our national legislature, and we call upon that body to act.

Congress has been appealed to before. Petitions have been sent in. Delegations have waited upon the committees and members. The President of the United States has called attention to this subject in his messages to Congress. The gory picture of this crying evil has repeatedly been placed before the legislative eye of the nation. But Congress has not acted – has not exercised its prerogative – has not discharged its plain duty.

That body needs a little more pressure from behind and it is part of the black man's burden to turn the pressure on.

When a people ask for the redress of grievance, the value of the demand is usually measured by the force that is behind it. The families of the Italians, who were murdered in New Orleans a few years ago, placed their case in the hands of the government of Italy. The United States promptly paid the indemnity demanded. This country paid over one hundred thousand dollars to the heirs of some Chinaman who were murdered in a Western town a number of years ago.

We come to the American people with a prayer for relief. We ask for the redress of grievances. We ask at the hands of the American government that same measure of protection that is accorded the Italian, the Chinaman or the other stranger within its gates.

In making this request let us tabulate some of the forces that are behind our demand, then follow them up with persistent demonstration till our needed redresses are granted.

In the elections of 1896, the colored voter held the balance of power and decided the political complexion of eight great States of the American Union.

These States sent eighty electors to the electoral college, who decided the Presidential contest of that year. These States are represented in congress by eighty members – a number sufficient to decide the fate of any measure that comes before that body.

These States are Maryland and Delaware on the Atlantic; California and Oregon on the Pacific; Ohio, Indiana, Kentucky and West Virginia in the interior. To this list have been added the States of Kansas and Nebraska by the elections of 1900.

This grand loyal belt, anchored on both oceans and spanning the continent, consists of over 250,000 colored voters, who ask for the redress of our grievances. Besides this, there are in other parts of the country over thirty congressional districts which the organized colored vote can control. Besides this there are in the rest of the Union over 1,500,000 colored voters more, making a total of 2,000,000 voters representing 10,000,000 citizens.

All of this vast moral and material force asks for the redress of our grievances. These redresses must come. No people can long be the capricious victims of lynch law whose votes decide the issue when a national ruler is elected.

Either the example set by South Carolina and several other Southern States, in disfranchising the colored man because his grandfather was not a voter, shall prevail all over this land; either the constitution shall be defiantly set aside or the fifteenth amendment stricken from its sections; either the threat made by Robert Toombs, way back in 1860, that he would call the roll of his slaves at the base of Bunker Hill monument shall be verified by his descendents killing colored men with impunity in any part of this country; or the colored man must receive the benefits of law, justice and protection, in the north, in the south, in the east and in the west.

One way or the other this thing must go. This country can't be part law and part mob rule. It must be all one or the other.

In the early part of my remarks I called your attention to the complaint of South Carolina in 1860. In her ordinance of secession South Carolina arraigned the North for disregarding laws of Congress, made especially to rivet the bonds of human slavery upon the American Republic.

South Carolina complained because a freedom-loving people had not yielded full compliance to the odious demands of the fugitive slave law; had not, as directed by this law, freely joined the pack to hunt down the poor Negro who, galled and exasperated by the grinding chains of slavery, had asserted his manhood to the extent of abandoning his master's oppressive yoke. And because Northern freeman had refused to stultify their conscience – had hesitated to bow to the arrogant demands of the insolent slave power, South Carolina and other States severed their connection with the republic, and tried to destroy the government of the United States, with the avowed purpose of erecting upon its ruins a government whose corner stone should be human chattel slavery.

Today the situation is somewhat reversed. Today the North arraigns the South for disregarding the laws of Congress made in the interest of protection, progress and liberty.

It arraigns the States of South Carolina, North Carolina, Alabama, Mississippi, Louisiana, and other Southern States, for violating the thirteenth amendment to the constitution and the laws of Congress made in pursuance thereof, by their heinous convict lease system. It arraigns these States for violating the fourteenth amendment by retaining taxation and representation without franchise. It arraigns these States for violating the fifteenth amendment by their efforts to disfranchise the colored man. It arraigns these States for violating the Fifth Amendment to the constitution for not suppressing that devastating torrent of arson, rapine, carnage and agony that trails its paths of desolation across the distressed lands of darkest America.

Today the North arraigns these States for these offenses; but with no threat of secession, no threat to disrupt the Union, to narrow its domain, to wrench stars from its banner or tear stripes from its flag.

But we arraign these States with the glorious promise, sacredly registered in the breasts of a sufficient number of patriotic Americans; to launch the star spangled banner, with numbers accumulating to its stars, and weight gathering to its stripes upon the breezes of eternity, as an enduring emblem of freedom, greatness and civilization; and justice and equal rights to all.

We come to the American people with a prayer for relief. We ask for the redress of grievances. We ask that these shall be better evidence of the guilt of our people charged with these heinous crimes, than the unsupported statements of the lyncher, whose hands are dripping with the blood of his victim. We ask the Northern newspaper, in its glaring head-lines, to report the lynched Negro as only charged with the crime till some evidence of his guilt is furnished; and not copy verbatim the false and damaging message from the lynchers who at best are cold-blooded, cowardly murderers.

A little while ago they lynched a colored man down in Georgia by their chivalrous process of burning at the stake, and then cutting the victim's body up into small pieces and passing them among the lynchers as souvenirs. One of the participators on this affair, with one of these ghastly and revolting mementoes in his pocket, sent out word that was telegraphed all over the North, that a colored man had murdered a white man who was defending the honor of his home; and then, before the victim was dead, had outrageously assaulted the wife in the dying man's presence.

This statement was false, but it was accepted by the Northern press and the Northern pulpit as literally true. No effort was made to ascertain the facts. No reporters were sent by our great newspapers to get the correct news. But the lyncher's statement went far and wide, and with it the howls of indignation from the press and pulpit against colored men that encouraged and justified just such deeds as that Georgia mob had committed.

The vast machinery of the press and the telegraph exerted itself to circulate the false statement of a red-handed murderer, but it took no steps to correctly present a matter that affected the moral standing of ten million American citizens.

The Afro-American Council of Chicago took hold of the matter. Its members did not believe that the facts relating to the Georgia lynching had been published. They came together and raised the money, and employed the best detective of the Pinkerton agency to be had. And they sent him down to Georgia to get the facts. He was down there a number of days, upon the very ground where the outrage had been committed, passing as a vender of hog cholera medicine.

The facts are that the white man who was killed was trying to defraud the colored man out of his wages. The colored man wanted the money he had eared. The white man refused to pay the money he owed. The two were quarreling about the matter.

The quarrel became hot; and to end it the white man got hold of his loaded shot gun. The colored man got hold of an ax. Just as the white man was about to pull the trigger the colored man hurled the ax with fatal aim. He then immediately fled from the vicinity. He offered no violence to the white woman whatever.

Whatever view is taken of the colored man's act, it certainly bore no resemblance to the revolting picture which the lyncher sent forth into the willing ears of the Northern press and the Northern pulpit, and missionary work upon this same press and this same pulpit, is a legitimate portion of the black man's burden.

We come to the American people with a prayer for relief. We ask for the redress of grievances. We ask to have removed that terrible nightmare of lynch law, mob violence and assassination that darkens with its miasmatic denseness, the valley and the plain, reduced to civilization by the toil of the black man.

We ask for that protection which the American flag promised us at York Town and at Appomattox. We ask for a national law that shall cause lynchings to be investigated and the offenders punished. We ask for such national laws as will arrest that terrible trail of fire, blood, steel and tears that stretches its ghastly length along the sunniest belts of the American Republic.

We ask these at the hands of the hands of the National Legislature, and if they are not lawful let the courts proclaim to the world that the United States Government cannot protect its citizens from torture and murder.

We ask these in the name of humanity and civilization; in the name of two million voters and ten million citizens; in the name of the great American Republic; and we ask these in the name of the Great God of the Universe.

THE FRIGHTFUL EXPERIENCE
OF
JULIUS GARDNER

A man who was actually lynched, Mr. Gardner is the only colored man who, having been accused of crime and arrested by a southern mob, has lived to relate his experience.

Written by: Irenas J. Palmer

AN ARKANSAS LYNCHING

As related by Mr. Gardner.

In giving the following account of part of my experience during a residence of a few years in the South, I have attempted to adhere strictly to the truth, and to state the facts concisely, unencumbered by sentiment or my opinions. There is much more that I could say in connection with this subject, but nothing perhaps has been omitted that is essential to convey an insight into that phase of Southern lawlessness with which I had an experience.

I am in possession of evidence which will strongly corroborate my statements, and I can furnish the address of several respectable white people, who reside in the locality where the events I relate transpired, whose testimony will substantiate my narrative.

The name of Landen Morgan is assumed for relations sake, but many persons who lived along the Little Red River of Arkansas during the nineties, will be able to identify the person whom I designate by that name.

My name is Julius Gardner. I was born in Franklin, Pa. In 1893 I went south. I was in Kentucky, Tennessee and Arkansas. I was in Bardwell, Kentucky, on July 8th, 1893. It was the day after C. J. Miller was lynched there. I will speak of that lynching later on.

In the same month I went to Arkansas. There I leased a little farm of about twenty acres, situated on a creek that empties into the Little Red River. My farm was a triangular shaped piece, with one point running down into the impassable part of a swamp.

My lease was for five years, and it gave me the privilege to purchase, which I intended to do.

Landen Morgan was my nearest neighbor. He was a white man and was reputed to be wealthy. His farm of many acres bounded my land on one side while the swamp bounded the other two sides.

Mr. Morgan was not at home much. He was interested in racing horses.

My first interview with him took place after I had been about a month in Arkansas. I disliked and distrusted him from the start; and it was clear that I did not impress him favorably. He was accustomed to treat colored men with insolence and he expected them to be cringing and subservient. I put up with his overbearing ways, but I could not, had I tried, have assumed the servile attitude which he expected.

It was not long before I began to realize that Morgan was my enemy. He began to make things very unpleasant for me. Difficulties arose over the line between our farms, and we disagreed about the only road leading to my premises, and there were other disputed points. I put up with his unjust treatment and did all that I could not to aggravate the situation.

My lease, as I have mentioned, gave me the right to purchase the land I occupied. I had intended to settle down in that locality and it became reported around that I had purchased the place and paid for it. Most of the people there believed such to be the case. Morgan was among that number, for on one occasion he made a proposition to buy my place. His price was so low that I could not entertain it, though the situation had already reached the stage where I was willing to make some sacrifices. It was not long after this before I learned that Morgan had declared that he would drive me out of the country.

Morgan had been sheriff of that county and he aspired to go to the legislature. He and I were of opposite political parties. I seldom took any hand in politics beyond going to the polls to vote and advising my neighbors to do the same; but on one occasion, when Morgan was canvassing for the nomination, I made the remark that I hoped that he would be nominated as I considered him an easy man to beat. That was the whole extent of my electioneering in that campaign.

My remark was repeated to Mr. Morgan; and when he failed to get the nomination from the convention of his party, he ascribed his defeat to my influence and intensified his hate against me.

He sought, on several occasions, to get me into a quarrel, but he always selected opportunities when the advantages were in his favor. With much inconvenience I avoided him. I always welcomed the arrival of the dates when he departed upon his career of horse racing and gambling.

A crisis in our relations was inevitable, however, and it came. But I lacked the mental equipment to comprehend that it was coming.

One afternoon in the summer of 1896, I had been out hunting and was returning home. As I was passing along the road I heard the screams of a female near by, and I went through the dense growth of bushes that skirted the highway, over into the adjoining field to investigate. There I came upon Morgan, who was seeking to take advantage of a little colored girl – a fourteen year old daughter of one of my neighbors.

It was not Morgan's first offense of that character. He was a source of terror to the colored maidens of that section.

As soon as I discovered that Morgan was not armed I concealed my rifle in the bushes. There was a prospect of a physical encounter.

But an armed colored man in conflict with an unarmed white man is the exact reverse of the prevailing code in the South – a code which no ordinary circumstance would induce me to disregard.

I interfered in the girl's behalf. Morgan became irate and blasphemous. He made threats and used vile language, but at length he departed to his home, which was not far away.

I started with the girl towards her home, which was about a mile distant. She had been out picking berries. She had seen Morgan riding by, but did not think she had been seen by him. A half hour later he had surprised her by stepping suddenly from a clump of bushes and grasping her by the arm.

We had not traveled half the distance to the girl's home when we heard the approach of a horseman. Looking back I saw Morgan riding rapidly towards us with a revolver in his hand. Morgan did not know that I was armed. He had returned to his home and procured the revolver, and was now in pursuit, with an intention which I instantly discovered. He would shoot me down without a moment's hesitation. He was that kind of a man.

Had I been alone I might have avoided him without difficulty; but I was encumbered by the frightened little girl whom I would not desert. As soon as I discerned Morgan's intentions I put a cartridge in my rifle and faced him. My opponent saw the movement, but he continued to advance. When I thought he was near enough, I took aim and commanded him to halt or put up his revolver.

He returned the weapon to the holster and rode past us uttering a volley of threats and curses.

"I'll see whether or not a peaceable citizen can ride along the highway without being halted by an armed nigger," was his parting ejaculation.

I stood well with a number of influential white men in that vicinity, and I had always endeavored to attend strictly to my own business. I was aware of the fact that colored men were frequently lynched in the South, simply because they were objectionable to some one, and on other frivolous pretexts, but I did not fully realize the situation. Morgan's last words kept ringing in my ears, but they failed to impress me with their terrible import.

I did not know the South then as I do now. The section in which I lived had not then been visited by the lynching scourge. After my affair with Morgan, I decided to leave the country. I did not apprehend any immediate harm, but I was becoming tired of the disagreeable relations with my neighbor, and I began to adjust my business interests with the view of moving away.

During the following two or three weeks, things moved along about as usual, with two notable exceptions. Two events transpired which clearly were warnings of what was being attempted; but I failed at the time to correctly interpret their meaning, especially the first one.

Early one morning, a party of five white men, equipped for a hunting trip, came to my house and engaged me to pilot them through the swamp. They desired to reach the hunting grounds beyond, and I was familiar with the only route they could safely take. The party was composed of wealthy Southerners. One of them was the son of a prominent Arkansas statesman. I accompanied the party. We were gone until the next day. The hunters, on their return, passed my house. It was about five o'clock in the afternoon when we arrived there.

Just before reaching my house we encountered seven white men gathered by the road side. One of them had a coat in his hand, and as I came up he said;

"Is that your coat?"

I answered in the affirmative, after examining the garment.

"Then you are the man we want."

"May I ask what you want of me?"

"You'll find out soon enough."

Just then two of the men came up with ropes to bind me. One of the hunters then asked for an explanation of the proceedings.

It was given. The man who held the coat said that a white woman had been assaulted by a Negro who was wearing that coat at the time, and whose description tallied with my appearance.

"When did this happen?" asked the hunter, who, by the way, was the son of the Arkansas statesman.

"A little before noon," was the answer.

"Where did it happen?"

"A little ways down the road."

"How did you get the coat?"

"The fellow was being pursued and he threw it away, either because it encumbered him or to escape identification. John came upon him in time to save the girl."

John was pointed out to the hunter.

John's story was that he was passing along the road when he heard screams. He hurried along and soon came upon the Negro, who was dragging a white girl to the side of the road. As soon as John appeared upon the scene, the Negro fled. John pursued, but the Negro escaped. In his flight he threw his coat away.

I had been made to understand that the hunters were my friends and that they would establish my innocence.

"Where is the injured girl?" was the hunter's next question.

"She was taken over to Morgan's house," was the answer by the man who held the coat.

John was interrogated. He was very sure that I was the assailant. He was at one time within fifty feet of that person. He could swear that the assailant had on the same pants that I then had on. I had got another coat and had changed hats he admitted.

After some further conversation we all adjourned to Morgan's house. I was taken there to be identified by the girl.

The girl was not quite sure that I was the man who attacked her. I resembled him strongly.

Morgan was acquainted with the statesman's son. After greetings and some common place conversation, attention was directed to me.

Morgan sought to persuade the girl to declare that I was actually the assailant. She finally stated that she was very much frightened and did not notice closely, but as near as she could tell I was the miscreant.

This seemed to satisfy Morgan. He stated that the sheriff had been sent for to take me to jail to await trial. He believed that the facts in the case, as they appeared, warranted such a course. He turned to the hunters for their opinion.

The statesman's son answered:

"Early yesterday morning this man started with us on a journey across the swamp. He was with us all day yesterday, all last night, and all day today up till now. When the girl was attacked he was with us on the other side of the swamp. We know that he is not guilty."

I could see that Morgan was surprised and chagrinned. He controlled himself, however, and after a moment replied:

"That puts an entirely different phase upon the case. I have known Mr. Gardner for several years, and I was loth to believe that he would be guilty of such a deed." Then to the men who were to take me in custody, he added:

"It will not be necessary to detain your prisoner any longer. You should be able, however, to hunt out the guilty person."

With this I was dismissed. I returned to my home, and in my heart, thanking the hunters who had saved me a period in jail, and the trouble of establishing my innocence.

It was a week later when the knowledge came to me that I would never have reached the jail. A party of lynchers were to intercept the sheriff and make short work of his prisoner.

I never learned who the girl was that was attacked, or how she come to be in that vicinity alone, but it was reported to me that the girl had stated that she knew the person who attacked her was a white man blacked up.

The coat which the assailant was wearing when he encountered the young woman, was a discarded garment that had been hanging in an open shed in the rear of my dwelling.

I think the girl was actually attacked, and at the time I believed that suspicion had been directed to me, solely because the miscreant was wearing my purloined coat. But as I revolved the matter in my mind the truth began to gradually dawn upon me. I was marked for the victim of a conspiracy.

I became very guarded in my movements and devoted my time to arranging to leave the country.

One night, four or five days after I had accompanied the hunters, I heard an unusual stamping noise in the rear of my house. It appeared to be in the building I used as a stable, but no animal was in there – my horse was running loose in the fields.

I arose and cautiously proceeded to the outbuilding. There I found a strange horse hitched to the manger with one of my halters. The animal was muddy and had been ridden some distance. I was able to determine that the horse had been in the stable less than an hour.

It was a great mystery to me how the horse had got there or why he had been left there and fastened with my halter. Then it occurred to me like a flash that it was a plot to make me appear as a horse thief.

I immediately released the horse and started him out upon the road. For the remainder of the night I watched my premises, but nothing unusual happened.

My conjecture was right. The horse had been left in my stable with the deliberate intention of making it appear that I had stolen it. The men who were to surprise me with the horse in my possession were on the road for that purpose when I turned the animal loose. They were to awaken a white man, who worked for Morgan, and were to bring him along to establish my guilt. They were defeated in their plot by meeting their horse loose in the road, over two miles from where I lived.

These facts came to me in a way that I knew they were correct. I was aroused to an understanding of the situation. I realized that I was in great danger. I had active enemies who were conspiring to encompass my destruction. Their first step was to get me into custody of an officer – a mob of lynchers was to do the rest.

The second attempt to make me the victim of a conspiracy had failed; but my enemies were persistent, and their third attempt, notwithstanding the warnings I had received, found me an easy victim.

One afternoon three or four days later, a man and a woman drove up to my abode. The woman wanted to purchase my farm. She said she had timber interests in the swamp which were to be developed, and that it would facilitate her business to occupy my premises. I stated the nature of my claim and the price for the improvements I had made. She considered my terms reasonable. She was then in a hurry but would call the next day to complete the bargain.

It was understood in that vicinity that a widow woman owned a large tract of land, including the swamp adjoining my premises, and the visit of this woman looked to me then as a proper business step. Then, for reasons already stated, I was anxious to realize upon my interests in that locality. Actuated by this anxiety I walked readily into the trap set for me.

The next day the woman came as agreed, but on foot and alone. She explained that an accident had happened to their conveyance which would delay her male escort for perhaps an hour. In the meantime I could show her where the line that separated my premises from Morgan's intercepted the highway. She would have occasion to show this point to the man who was managing her lumber interests.

Everything appeared proper to me, and we started out for the purpose indicated. After walking along the road for a few minutes – she on one side and I on the other – she stopped suddenly and gazed intently upon the ground, at the same time calling me to her. I crossed the road, and as soon as I got near enough, she threw her arms about my neck and shouted, "Murder! Murder! Take him away!"

I thought the woman was crazy; and as she began to sink to the ground, I caught her to support her. Just then three white men stepped from the bushes into the road and came up to us. Two of the men were unknown to me. The other worked for Morgan.

As they came up the woman accused me of assault, and the men strongly corroborated her assertion.

The men took charge of me. Two of them held pistols to my head, while the other bound me, hand and foot. In a little while the woman's escort drove up and with her drove away.

The three men started with me towards the swamp. We had gone but a short distance when five or six more white men appeared upon the scene. We were in a sparsely settled country. There were not half a dozen white families within a radius of four miles.

But within an hour from the time of my arrest I was surrounded by more than thirty white men, all armed, and in a country where it would have taken at least ten hours to assemble that number. There were not more than two or three of them whom I had ever met before.

As the crowd kept increasing the situation was explained to each fresh arrival, by accusing me of a dastardly crime; by stating that my victim was barely alive and that a carriage had to be procured to carry her away. Downright falsehoods and distortions of the truth used in profusion.

It did me no good to declare my innocence; for me to declare that the woman had not been injured in the least, and that she had gone away in the same carriage that had brought her. It did me no good to challenge them to produce the injured woman, or to give me the benefits of an investigation. I charged them with conspiracy. I accused them of having planned the outrage at least ten hours before

I was arrested. I pointed out the fact that so many men could not possibly have been assembled in the hour and a half that had passed since I was walking along the road with the woman, unless the affair had been pre-arranged. But all that I could say did no good. The answers I got were curses and blows.

There was, however, one just man in that gathering. He knew that I was innocent. But for his presence my name would have been one more to add to the list of thousands of innocent victims of Southern lawlessness. He was an entire stranger to me then. I afterwards learned that he was a government officer, and that he was then engaged in trailing down a gang of illicit whiskey manufacturers who were operating in that county.

It was near night-fall when we reached the edge of the swamp. I was not ignorant of the fate intended for me. I was to be lynched. The mob was now about fifty strong.

They were debating the question whether I should be lynched by hanging or burning. Those who came latest favored burning; but some of those who knew I was entirely innocent would have been contented with hanging.

While the question was being debated, three men came up to me – one of them had a rope. He instructed the other two to stand back and catch the end of the rope as he threw it over a limb. After this was accomplished he proceeded to fasten the rope about my neck.

His language was insulting, and his actions were threatening toward me. While he was fastening the rope he caught hold of me and wrenched me around with a force that nearly threw me to the ground. While he was doing this, he managed to say to me in a whisper:

"I will free your hands and give you a knife. Don't move until I am away from you, then get a gun and scoot."

With this he freed my hands, leaving a knife in my possession. He accomplished this without being observed by any of the gathering. Then he finished tying one end of the rope about my neck, and addressing the men who held the other end, said:

"Just keep a hand there boys, an when yer git the signal, just haul that nigger up like yer meant business."

His frontier dialect was assumed. His whispers to me were in good English.

He then went over to where most of the men were gathered, discussing the method of lynching.

My attention was directed to this man when he first came upon the scene. About a dozen men had gathered before he arrived. He took a hand in the direction of affairs at once, but every act and word of his showed that he had an intense hatred for colored people. It was he who caused my captors to halt at a cross-road for twenty minutes to receive a delegation that did not come. It was he who first suggested burning as the punishment I should receive. He succeeded in delaying the execution for nearly an hour in order to procure a chain and a can of oil. He was responsible for other delays. It was all plain to me now. He was maneuvering for time and the approach of night to facilitate my escape.

He was closely watching the impulses that controlled the situation. He knew just where to yield to those who were in favor of hanging, and at just the right moment he picked up the rope and came up to me, saying: "I kinder think burnin' is the proper medicine, but if it's to be hangin, let's be ready. We'll first git the rope fixed an then I want to say a dozen words, an then I'm ready fer the vote."

He had volunteered to fasten the rope about my neck, ostensibly to show that he was with the majority, but in reality because it gave him the opportunity to start me on the path of escape.

The revulsion of feelings, consequent upon the promise of escape which had come to me so unexpectedly, nearly unmanned me. It was several seconds before I felt myself under control. I might have used more time in steadying myself, but the debate as to the method of lynching had come to a sudden close, and the lynchers, impatient of delay, had started for the rope.

I had no time to lose. My first act was to cut the cords that bound my ankles. This movement was noticed and the alarm was given. Instantly the men surged upon the rope and I was swung into midair.

In the same breath in which the alarm was given, I seized the rope above my head with my left hand.

I was raised three or four feet from the ground before I could cut it with my other hand. As I dropped to the ground I caught up a shot gun that leaned against the tree that was to do duty as a stake or a gallows, and sprang to the cover of a thicket three or four rods away. The shot gun had a belt fastened to it filled with cartridges. It had been designedly left there, as I learned later on.

I was out of sight before any of the lynchers could turn their guns on me, and had turned sharply to one side in time to avoid the shots that were poured into the thicket at the point where I had disappeared.

The enemy did not evince any disposition to follow me into the thicket. As soon as they could realize the situation they began to seek cover. I could easily have inflicted injury upon some of them, but I had already decided to do no more than would be needed to insure my escape.

The gathering darkness was in my favor. It lent a gloom to the vicinity a short distance from the pine knot fire, which was to illuminate a burning or a hanging that did not invite rash pursuit of a fugitive, equipped with a gun and ammunition, and the resolution to use them if the situation demanded it.

The lynchers were without blood hounds, otherwise I should have been speedily recaptured. I knew that it would require several hours to procure the animals.

The natural impulse of a man, just escaped from my predicament, would be to put distance between himself and his enemies as rapidly as possible; and this is just what my foes decided that I would do. But to do this would be to plunge into the impassable bogs and mire of the swamp, and invite certain recapture. I was thoroughly familiar with the country. My path of escape lay close to a line which I knew my enemies would instantly guard. I decided on this course and it proved my salvation.

I was none too soon, either. While traversing this path I came close to two or three of the lynchers who had evidently kept in the background. Morgan was one of the number. He had just been informed of my escape. He did not believe that I had retreated into the swamp, and he gave directions to have men stationed in a position, which, if it had been adopted in time, would have cut off my escape. I succeeded in eluding them, however, and hurried towards my home. A few minutes later I was arrested by the question: "Did you get the gun and scoot?" At the same time my benefactor stepped from the bushes in front of me, I recognized him at once. In reply to his questions I told him that it was a mile and a half to my house and that I desired to go there to get money and weapons, and that I had decided to leave the country immediately.

"Your plan is all right except going to your home. There will be men there to receive you. I will get your money and your weapons and will meet you at Sandy Ford as soon as you can get there."

Three-quarters of an hour later I met the government officer at Sandy Ford. We had a conversation lasting nearly an hour. He explained why he had exerted himself to save my life. First, because it was an act of humanity. Second, I knew that Morgan was interested in the illegal manufacture of whiskey, and Morgan knew that I knew it. The officer while shadowing the whiskey men had overheard the plot to get rid of me because I knew too much about the illegal whiskey business. There was a possibility that my evidence would be needed in the government courts on this account.

After parting with the officer, I crossed the river. I succeeded in making my way to Chicago. I abandoned what interest I had in the Arkansas property, and have never been South since.

Since that time I have investigated the lynching scourge to some extent, and I am actually horrified at its extent and its fiendishness, and the absence of justification. My information has been derived largely from the published reports, and I shall not consume much of your time in rehearsing the accounts of outrages, that have from time to time been laid before the American people in the public prints.

Colored people are lynched in the South for the following crimes and offenses: Rape, alleged rape, and suspected rape. For murder, alleged murder, or suspected murder. For larceny, alleged or suspected. For arson, actual, alleged or suspected. For poisoning stock or wells, or being accused of such crime. For self defense, for insulting whites, and for turning State's evidence. For being related to a criminal or to a person charged with crime, and for refusing to disclose the whereabouts of a criminal.

For wife-beating; for being acquitted by a white jury; for race prejudice, and for no offense at all. A colored man is guilty of a crime, so far as lynching purposes are required, by simply being accused by any white man; a colored person's testimony is always sufficient to convict a colored man, though it is valueless in all other respects. No other evidence is needed to encompass the death of a colored person in the South, than to be accused of crime by a white man, and the report always goes out and is accepted, that the victim was guilty as charged.

I will recite the accounts of two or three cases of Southern lynchings, which have been proven by the testimony of some of the best white people living in the vicinity where the outrages occurred.

The fourteen year old daughter and the sixteen year old son of a man named Hastings were hanged, and their bodies riddled with bullets, because their father had been accused of murdering a white man. The father was afterwards lynched. This was November 1892, at Jonesville, Louisiana.

Five persons, Benjamin Jackson, his wife, his mother-in-law, Louis Carter and Rufus Bigley, were lynched near Quincy, Miss. In September, 1892. The charge was well-poisoning. A family named Woodruff was taken ill, and it was surmised that the illness was caused by poison that had been put in their well. It was never shown that this was the cause of the sickness and it was never shown that any poison had been put in the well. It was surmised that Benjamin Jackson had put poison in the well. He was arrested, and without any investigation whatever, with the other four persons named, was lynched.

John Peterson, near Denmark, South Carolina, was suspected of rape. He escaped from his captors, and he had an excellent opportunity to escape from the country. But he was an innocent man, and he felt that he would receive fair treatment by surrendering to the highest authorities in the State. He surrendered to Governor Tillman and couted the strictest investigation. He asserted that all he asked was an opportunity to prove a complete alibi by white witnesses. A white reporter, hearing the declarations, volunteered to find these witnesses. He informed the Governor that he would have them at the executive mansion in twenty-four house. This respite was not granted by Governor Tillman. He freely surrendered the prisoner to the Denmark mob. The prisoner was taken back for identification. The injured girl positively declared that Peterson was not the guilty man. It did no good. Peterson was hanged and his body riddled with bullets. Another report went out of the lynching of a black fiend.

I have no taste for these recitals, I assure you. They are presented for the sole purpose of arraying the truth before the American people.

I have not selected exceptional cases. My recitals refer to average samples. Press reports of Southern lynchings always emanate from the lyncher or his sympathizer; but even these reports are damnable enough.

In a county in Mississippi, during the month of July, 1892, the Associated Press dispatches reported that a big black burly brute had assaulted the eight year old daughter of the sheriff and that the brute had been promptly lynched.

The facts, which have since been investigated, show that the girl was almost twenty years old, and that the "brute" was a year younger and was a servant in the family. The girl was discovered by her father in the young man's room, where she had been a clandestine visitor for more than a year.

A Negro boy was lynched in Tuscumbia, Alabama, the same year, and on the same charge. It was shown that he and the girl had been meeting in the woods by appointment for several months.

There is a young mulatto in one of the State prisons of the South, today, who is there by the charge of a young white girl to screen herself. He is a college graduate and had been corresponding with and clandestinely visiting her until he was surprised and run out of her room en dishabille by her father. He would have been promptly lynched, but he threatened to show the letters which the young woman had written him. To escape lynching he plead guilty and was sent to prison.

One more case will close my accounts of Southern lawlessness.

Wednesday, July 5th, 1893, a terrible crime was committed a short distance from Wickliff, Kentucky. Two girls, Marry and Ruby Ray, were found murdered a short distance from their homes. The news of the crime spread like wild fire, and searching parties were speedily organized to hunt down the villain who had committed the dastardly deed. Some one saw a white man fleeing from the vicinity of the outrage, but he escaped. The search continued all day, but without results. A blood hound was brought from the penitentiary and put upon the trail which he followed to the river and into the boat of a fisherman. The fisherman stated that he had ferried only one man across the river on July 5th, and that was a white man. The hound was taken across the river, and struck the trail again at Bird's Point, on the Missouri side, and ran about three hundred yards to the house of a white man. The animal then refused to go farther.

The next day a brakeman on a freight train going out of Sikeston, Mo., had a fight with a Negro who was stealing a ride. The Negro was arrested. The Sikeston authorities jumped to the conclusion that they had captured the murderer of the two girls, and they sent word to the Bardwell authorities to that effect. The same day the authorities of Sikeston, Mo., turned the prisoner over to a Kentucky mob and he was taken to Bardwell.

A funeral pyre had been erected in the middle of the village, and while the crowd was clamoring for the prisoner's life, he stepped forward and said:

"My name is C.J. Miller. I live at No. 716 N. 2nd St. Springfield, Illinois. I am not guilty of this crime. I was never in the State of Kentucky till you brought me here.

When the girls were killed I was on the cars riding from Memphis to Jonesborough. I can prove this by the conductor of that train."

A telegram was sent to the chief of police of Springfield, asking if one C.J. Miller lived there. An affirmative answer was received, but it came after the victim had been lynched.

The father of the murdered girls was satisfied that the murderer was a white man. There was not one particle of evidence – even circumstantial evidence – pointing to Miller's guilt. All the evidence pointed to a white man as the villain.

But it made no difference. Miller was dragged through the streets of Bardwell with an iron chain around his neck, and was hanged to a telegraph pole. His body was afterwards burned on the spot.

I was in Bardwell the day after the lynching. The chain still hung from the cross-arm of the telegraph pole, and the ashes of the cremation still littered the streets. I was told that a black desperado, who had murdered two white girls, had been lynched. Had I been put in possession of the facts of the case, my stay in the South would have ended there and then.

It is not claimed that no colored men are guilty of the crimes charged against them, but the records show that reasonable proof of guilt has been established against less than twelve out of a hundred of those who have been murdered. Colored men have committed crimes that deserve the severest punishment. No country has ten million inhabitants without some of them being criminals.

The Negro of the South sees the womanhood of his race assailed by white men with impunity. He sees colored men deprived of life, liberty and property, without due process of law. He sees colored men hung, shot or burned to death, when he knows the victims are innocent. He realizes that there is no premium on innocence; that the innocent suffer and the guilty escape. An honest, upright colored man and a scoundrel are equally exposed to the fatal accusation of a white man.

How far a spirit of retaliation, or contempt for abortive law, is responsible for the criminal deeds of colored men, must, however, remain a matter of speculation.

There is no excuse for lynch law in the South. The judges, the juries, the courts, the officers, are white men. The whole machinery of the law and the government is in the hands of white men. The jurors and the officers are selected from the same class that furnish the men who tie the halter, draw the shot gun, or apply the match. No guilty colored man can possibly escape the verdict of a Southern court. The miserable subterfuge that legal trials are dispensed with only in cases of assault, and then because it would wound the feelings of the injured female to appear in court as a witness, betrays its hollowness when it is shown that only about thirty-eight out of every four hundred colored men lynched in the South, are even charged with the crime of rape. The other excuse offered, that lynchings mostly occur in the sparsely settled districts, where the machinery of the law is not in effective operation, is flatly contradicted by the records, which show that eight out of ten of all the lynchings occur in or near the cities or organized towns and that they are generally witnessed by thousands of spectators.

There is a remedy, of course, for this deplorable condition of things. It is a well established principle that every wrong has a remedy. But the South will never evolve it. The remedy will be applied, however, but it must be by the progressive and order-respecting forces of the nation. I will offer, in closing, just one suggestion, which, when adopted, will do much towards removing the scourge which darkens the South and smirches the nation.

Let the law–respecting element of the country condemn, in the severest terms, the lyncher in every case as a cold-blooded, cowardly murderer, and let it vigorously denounce every case of human punishment that is not the result of a legal trial.

I.J. Palmer: February 20, 1902.